A WORD FROM THE AUTHOR

FALASHA NO MORE is for children and parents who want to learn more about the modern challenges and age-old Judaic customs of Israel's newest citizens, the Jews of Ethiopia. It is the story of an Ethiopian family struggling to reconcile their own ancient Jewish customs with today's Israeli society. I hope that FALASHA NO MORE will touch all those, Jews and non-Jews alike, who care for the fate of their fellow human beings around the globe.

While living in Israel, I was most fortunate to come to know many Ethiopian Jews. They revealed to me the poignant, often bitter truths of the persecution they suffered in their lives in Ethiopia, their deep desire to become part of a new Jewish society and their understandable difficulties in doing so. Nevertheless, all of them have high hopes and dreams for a wonderful future in Israel.

I was captivated by their humanity, dignity and strength, and I found myself quickly drawn to them. The Jews of Ethiopia have been battered and abused for the last two thousand years, yet they still cling to their old ways with fierce devotion, determined at the same time to belong to the contemporary world of Israel.

The theme that runs through FALASHA NO MORE is universal: The essential value of human beings transcends all cultural differences. If a child reads these pages and comes away with a heightened appreciation of what it means to be "different," if he understands that all people have the right to be accepted and loved for what they are, then I have achieved my intention in writing this book.

To learn to take pride in one's unique heritage is an integral part of growing up healthy. FALASHA NO MORE acquaints young readers with the exodus of Ethiopian Jews and with the joy and pain of developing one's personal identity in a sometimes hostile world.

FALASHA NO MORE:

An Ethiopian Jewish Child Comes Home

by Arlene Kushner

Illustrations by
Amy Kalina

A Shapolsky Book
Published by Shapolsky Books
a division of
Steimatzky Publishing of North America, Inc.

For any additional information, contact Steimatzky Publishing of North America, Inc., 56 East 11th Street, NY, NY 10003.

Cover design by Mike Stromberg
Typography by Type Network (KTN)

10 9 8 7 6 5 4 3 2 1

1st Edition January 1986

ISBN 0-933503-55-5

Library of Congress Cataloging in Publication Data
Kushner, Arlene—1986
    Falasha No More: An Ethiopian Jewish Child Comes Home

STEIMATZKY
SHAPOLSKY
NEW YORK • JERUSALEM • TEL AVIV

My name is Avraham—Avraham Tesfa Fereday. I am a black-skinned Jew and I have come from Ethiopia. Thousands of my people have come. It has been very difficult for us. But we are in our homeland now: we are in Israel.

I am with my family. My Mama is here, and my Papa, and my brother Getu, and my little sister Almaz. When we first came to Israel we were very excited.

Now we have learned Hebrew, and Papa has found work. This night we are also excited. It is our first night in our own new apartment. We sit and we talk.

"It will not be difficult for us," Papa says. "Now we are all Jews together. Soon our people will be at home here." His words make me think about how wonderful it will be when I am really Israeli.

Papa keeps talking. "But just because we are here doesn't mean that we should forget, children. We have suffered to be Jewish; our people have been beaten and killed. Do you remember how the others in Ethiopia said that Jews are bad luck? They called us 'Evil-eye.'"

"Buda! Buda!" Getu cries out. He is saying the Ethiopian word for "Evil-eye." And then Almaz points a finger at me and frowns. *"Falasha!"* she hisses, using the Ethiopian word which means stranger.

Papa nods. "You children do remember," he says. "But no more *Buda* here, no more *Falasha*." He sits up very straight in his chair, and smiles slowly.

"In Israel we are one people," Papa says. "Here no one is *Falasha*, no Jew is a stranger. Do you also remember the feelings we had about Israel when we were in Ethiopia?"

"Zionism, Papa," I say.

"What?" Papa asks.

"Zionism is the word for the feeling about Israel," I tell him.

"Ah," says Papa. "A new word. But an old feeling. I remember how my grandfather used to tell me that some day we would go to Jerusalem."

Papa sighs deeply. He puts his hands up against his chest. "It brings me pain to think about this," he tells me, "because grandfather did not live to come with us. But it is because of what he taught me that we are here today."

Mama looks at me, and at Almaz and Getu. "You are tired, children," she says. "It has been a long day. Go to bed now."

Almaz and Getu go. I really do not feel like it, because I am still excited. I obey Mama anyway, and I get into my bed. At first sleep does not come. And in the kitchen I hear Mama and Papa still talking.

"After all of these years," Papa is saying, "we have finally come to this happy time. Think of it. For over two thousand years in Ethiopia we lived by the rules of the Torah. We can be proud. We have kept the Shabbat and the Jewish Festivals. And now we are in our holy land of Israel."

Now Mama is speaking. Her voice is very low. I cannot hear what they are saying anymore. I begin to sleep.

And I have a dream: We have been walking in the desert for hours and my parents are getting farther and farther away from me. My throat is very dry, but our water container is gone. The bandits called *shifta* have taken it. I am terrified. The sun is blinding. I can hear my parents calling out to me, "Avraham! Avraham!"

Suddenly it is morning. The sun is shining brightly into my room, right onto my face. It is a hot Israeli sun. I sit up and look out the window. What I see in the distance are the mountains of Israel. They are very different from the Ethiopian mountains I remember.

A loud horn goes BEEP — and I jump. A bus is driving by on the street in front of our apartment. In our village in Ethiopia the loudest sound I heard in the morning was the soft "baaa" of the sheep being herded up the hillside near our home.

"Avraham!" Mama calls, "Come! Did you forget that you begin school today?"

School! There is a sick feeling in my stomach. I am frightened about this new school and the new people. Mama must rush me. She serves me breakfast and sends me out the door.

15

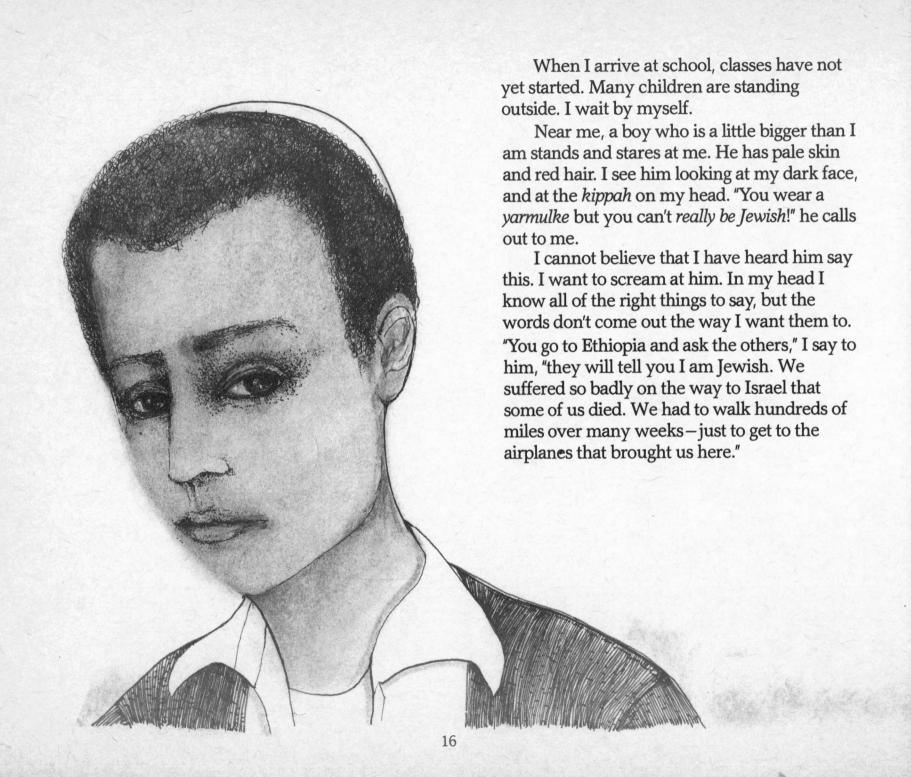

When I arrive at school, classes have not yet started. Many children are standing outside. I wait by myself.

Near me, a boy who is a little bigger than I am stands and stares at me. He has pale skin and red hair. I see him looking at my dark face, and at the *kippah* on my head. "You wear a *yarmulke* but you can't *really be Jewish!*" he calls out to me.

I cannot believe that I have heard him say this. I want to scream at him. In my head I know all of the right things to say, but the words don't come out the way I want them to. "You go to Ethiopia and ask the others," I say to him, "they will tell you I am Jewish. We suffered so badly on the way to Israel that some of us died. We had to walk hundreds of miles over many weeks—just to get to the airplanes that brought us here."

16

"Then I look down at the ground because tears are coming into my eyes. When I look up, the boy is gone. I feel like a stranger, and it is very hard for me to walk into the classroom when school begins. It is November. All the others have been in this school for months already. I want to run the other way, but my feet take me inside.

18

ק ר ץ

The children in my new class all stare at me. But the teacher is friendly and smiles. Her voice is very nice.

"Avraham is new here," she tells the students. "He comes from the Semien Mountains in Ethiopia." She points to a map. "It is beautiful there and the climate is mild.

"Once, a long time ago, the Jews in Ethiopia had their own kingdom. There was an Ethiopian Jewish king named Gideon and a queen named Judith. But the other Ethiopians destroyed the Jewish kingdom in a war, and said that the Jews could not own land anymore. For hundreds of years the Jews had to do work on farms they could only rent. At most they had a few cattle or sheep of their own. So you can see that Avraham and his people had a hard life in Ethiopia. Many are poor there, but the Jews are among the poorest of all."

Then the teacher says she wants to teach a special lesson, the one that she saves for new students from different lands. She begins to talk about flowers. "A garden is more beautiful when it has many kinds of flowers in it, " she says. "Each flower has a different job to do. One grows tall, while another grows low. Some flowers have beautiful smells. Some have wonderful shapes and some have marvelous colors. But how can you say that one flower is better than the other? They are all good. They are all part of the family of flowers in the garden.

"Our land of Israel is like a garden. And all of our children from different faraway places are like wonderful flowers — children like Avraham and Zev and Shira. They are all valuable.

21

I listen to the teacher, but her words do not make sense to me. The boy sitting next to me sees the confusion on my face. "This teacher says things like that," he whispers to me. "Don't worry . . . after a while you will understand the meaning of what she is saying."

Now the teacher turns and begins to write numbers on the blackboard, but the boy continues to whisper to me. "My name is Zev. When I came here from Argentina last year, I spoke only Spanish. Shira, over there, came from the Soviet Union a few months ago. Each time a new student arrives in our class the teacher tells this flower story. I know how you feel. I was confused in the beginning. But it really does make sense after a while."

During recess all of the children go outside. Zev goes with me, and I can see that others are watching us. "Are you ready for Chanukah?" Zev asks me.

"Chanukah?" I ask him. "I guess this is something I will have to learn about here."

"You're joking!" Zev says. "Everyone knows about Chanukah. In Argentina I knew." Nearby a group of boys begin listening.

"Some of our customs are different in Ethiopia," I say.

"Different from Chanukah?" Zev asks.

"Yes," I answer. But we do celebrate Seged." I hear the boys laughing at me.

"Seged?" Zev asks. "Who ever heard of Seged?"

"My people, the Jews of Ethiopia," I tell him. "It is our special holiday. We fast and then have prayers on the mountain. After this, we have a feast."

"No kidding," says Zev. "Is this what your rabbi says you should do?"

"We don't have rabbis," I tell him.

"Now I know that you're joking," Zev says. "All Jews have rabbis."

"No," I say. "We are Jews, but we have a *kes* instead of a rabbi."

"*Kes?*" Zev asks.

"Oh, excuse me," I say. "I forgot that you don't understand. *Kes* is a word in Amharic, my language from Ethiopia. It means a *Kohain*, a Jewish priest. You know, like the priests in Jerusalem's great Temple a long time ago."

Zev nods. "Oh, I see," he tells me. He goes to join the other boys who have been listening all this time. They have silly smiles on their faces.

Zev talks softly to three of his friends. "Why can't he be with us?" I hear him say. His voice sounds angry. Finally they all walk over to me.

"Avraham," says one of the boys, named Dani, "we are meeting in the park at the bottom of the hill at two-thirty this afternoon. You can come too."

"Thank you," I say. "I will be there."

I go home and tell Mama about my first day at school. I have something to eat, before starting out for the park. It is a beautiful day and I do not want to rush. When you rush you miss many good things. I slow down to look at some clouds in the sky and a bird in the tree.

Then I see Mrs. Tov, who lives in the apartment next to ours, and stop to talk to her. It feels good to talk to people. Besides, it would be rude to leave her too quickly, so we speak for a long time.

When I get to the park, the boys are not there. I ask a man for the time. "Three-forty-five," he says.

"Oh," I realize, "I must be too late." I walk home slowly.

The next day all the boys are angry with me. "Avraham," they yell, "what is the matter with you?"

"I am sorry," I say softly. "I promise to try harder next time."

"I hope you will," says Dani.

I'm learning," I answer. "I want to be a good friend."

"Don't good friends show up on time?" Dani asks. "I hope you realize that we waited for you."

I feel afraid inside because I see that Dani does not understand me. I am not sure he cares about understanding me. I know that I am trying.

Zev is standing next to me. I talk to him, because Zev tries to understand. "In Ethiopia we do not live by clocks so much," I say. "I think maybe you miss many important things if you worry about time too much."

Everyone is listening to me. I become very brave and keep talking. "My father can look at any plant and tell you many things about it. He can tell what it is, how it grows and if it is safe to eat. My father does not read many books. But he is a wise man, because he understands so many things. I am young. Yet even I know about wild animals, because they were living near our home. And I also know secret ways to walk through the woods without ever getting lost."

"Wow! Don't you wish you knew some of these things?" Zev asks the others. They don't answer, but they are not laughing.

I suddenly realize how much I have talked, and I stop. I see in the boys' faces that they are not angry at me anymore, and I am happy. I am Ethiopian, but suddenly I also want to be Israeli with them. The longing is very strong inside of me. I want to be both at the same time.

No one speaks. I am so nervous that I can hear myself swallowing.

Zev comes over and slaps my shoulder hard. "Speak up, Avraham," he calls out loudly. "You are so quiet. Don't be afraid. It's a free country." The slap frightens me for a moment, but I know that Zev is being kind. This is just his way.

"I hear your words, Zev, but until now I have never been free," I explain. "Life in Ethiopia was hard, and so many were against the Jews. We had a synagogue once, but it was closed by the army. We have learned to hold our thoughts inside. It is hard for me to change."

"You are so polite," one of the boys shouts. "Do you think your Ethiopian ways are better?"

I shrug. "For me it is better to say things slowly and carefully. Sometimes your loudness and directness confuse me. Maybe one way of behaving is not better than the other—but what is certain is that we are different."

As I say this I realize I am an Ethiopian. The Israeli boys don't know what else to say to me. They turn and leave. Suddenly I remember the teacher's lesson about the flowers. I want to call to the boys, to tell them that even though we are different, we can still be friends. But I don't know how to do this. The feelings are too strong inside of me. I cannot explain it the way the teacher did. I say nothing, and the boys walk away.

For days I am silent. Mama worries about me. She asks me if I am sick, and I tell her that I am okay. I want to tell my parents what is wrong, but I cannot. Mama and Papa think that I am becoming Israeli. I am sad because I know that they will be disappointed in me.

One morning Mama says to me, "Why don't you invite your new friends here for an Ethiopian meal?" Although I smile at her as I run out the door, what she has said makes me feel even worse. I don't have any friends to invite.

In school I keep to myself. I see that the boys look at me, but I do not know how I should behave so that I can be their friend. In Ethiopia I would know how to act.

One day, Zev leans over to me in class and asks, "How is your family?"

I am surprised that he is interested in my family. "They are fine, thank you," I answer. Suddenly I feel better, stronger.

After class is over, I see the three boys standing together, with Zev. I know it is a good time to do what Mama said. I go to them and find the courage inside me to say, "I want to invite all of you to come to my home for dinner today – at five." Then I hold my breath.

The boys look at each other, and say nothing. For a moment I think I have made a serious mistake.

Then Zev says, "I will be there, it sounds like fun!" And the others say, "Me too." I am happier now than I have been in many days.

By the time it is five, my family and I are ready for our
guests. I am very nervous. I hear them knock on the door and
I open it. They walk in slowly, and I see that they are
also nervous.

Papa comes forward to welcome them. For
each boy he holds out his hands in a clasp of
greeting, and he bows. The boys look at
each other. Their eyes are wide. They have
never seen this type of Ethiopian greeting.

Mama comes forward and she kisses each boy. First on one cheek and then on the other. Then again on the first cheek and also on the other. I hear two of the boys giggle quietly, and I begin to think maybe I shouldn't have invited them. But I will not be ashamed of my Ethiopian parents and our different customs.

"Come, come," Papa says. "You must wash and sit down to eat something." As he says this, I become nervous about our different food.

In our village in Ethiopia we lived in a hut made of straw and mud, called a *tukel*. We were very poor and we didn't have much, but we shared and it was all right. I remember

that once an American man came to our house and saw that we had only a little to eat and did not want to take from us. I think that maybe he was a kind man. But father was insulted. My people are proud, and sharing is important to us. I do not want this to happen again now, with the Israeli boys.

They sit with my family at the table. Dani looks at the food. "What is this?" he asks me.

"This is called *injera*," I tell him. It is our form of bread, made like a big floppy pancake. "We don't use forks," I explain. "We do this." I break off a piece of *injera* and use it to scoop up some of Mama's chicken stew. The boys all watch me.

"Our food is spicy," I say. "Except the *injera*. It is plain so that it can soak up the flavor of the sauce."

Dani tries. "This is good!" he declares. The others try. Mama smiles. Papa smiles. And I also smile.

We finish eating. Mama then clears the table and serves tea. We sit and talk.

"What is that?" Zev asks. He points to a woven basket of many colors hanging on the wall.

"Almaz," I say to my little sister, "go and take it off the wall and bring it here for my friends."

Almaz gets up and does as I ask her.

"I don't believe it," Ron says out loud. "My little sister would call me a donkey and tell me to go get it myself."

I laugh. "It is our way. The younger one must obey the older."

"Hey," Dani says. "That's great for the older one, like you. But what happens if you're the younger one, like me?"

"Well," I tell him, "it is up to me to help my little sister and take care of her."

I take the basket from my sister Almaz. "My mother made this," I tell the boys. "In our culture many women do this craft."

"Your mother is talented," Ron says.

I think to myself how very proud I am of her.

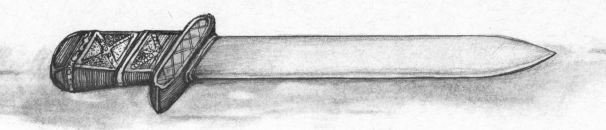

Ron picks up a specially made knife that is on the table. "This looks interesting," he says. "Where did it come from?"

"My uncle made it," I tell him. "In Ethiopia, it was our Jewish people who did metal work. They made jewelry, plows, and many other tools. And they were so skilled that they were famous throughout the country. Many years ago, when Ethiopian kings wanted metal work done, they called for Jews, who do it best of all."

"Wow!" the boys all call out.

Mama touches my shoulder. Papa puts his arm around me.

"People in your family touch a lot, don't they?" asks Dani.
I smile. "Yes," I say to him. "My brother Mehari is close to me this way too."

"You have a brother named Mehari?" Zev asks. "I didn't know that."

"Well," I explain, "I do . . . but I don't. It is different in our culture. My father has a brother. And this brother has a son, who is Mehari. You would call him a cousin. I call him brother because he is as close as a brother.." It is strange that I must explain this, because I feel the love of a brother for Mehari and that should be enough. But I am in Israel, not Ethiopia and here the customs are different.

Mama leans over to Papa. "Tesfa Fereday," she says to him, "would you like more tea?"

"Please, yes." Papa smiles.

David is listening closely. "Your father's name is Tesfa Fereday?" he asks me.

"That's right," I say. "Tesfa Fereday Wote."

"I think I am confused," David says. "Your name is Avraham Tesfa Fereday, isn't it?"

"That's right," I answer. I begin to laugh because I understand his confusion. "My father is Tesfa and Fereday was his father, and Wote was his grandfather. I am Avraham, and Tesfa is my father and Fereday was my grandfather. You see? That is how we get our names."

"How else should we call ourselves?" Papa asks. "This is our custom. It is the way of the Bible."

David thinks hard. "And your mother?" he asks.

"She is Rahel Wonede Mengistu," I tell him.

"But she doesn't have the same last name as your father," David says.

"How would anyone know about my family if I took the names of my husband's family?" Mama asks.

"You are right, Mama," I tell her. "But there is also another way of doing this. In Israel, a husband and wife and children all have the same family name." She nods. And I feel very excited because I see for the first time that I can explain new customs. I am now beginning to feel like an Israeli.

Mama serves more tea and fruit. We sit around the table and talk for a long time. Our voices are soft. We laugh and we touch.

Papa talks to the boys. "You know," he says, "our young people are very eager to learn. My brother's son, Mehari, he is already studying at the University in Tel Aviv.

"I think in time all of our youngsters will learn to be Israeli. This is good. Some day they will be just like you, and we will all be the same here in Israel."

I love my father very much. It is hard for me to disagree with him. I must show respect. "Papa," I say slowly, "my teacher in school has taught me something. Our culture is like a flower. How can it be good if all the flowers in the garden are the same?"

I am trying to be careful in the way I speak to Papa. I am being gentle, but Papa does not understand what I mean to say.

"Our culture is very special, I want to be Israeli. But I don't want to be just like everyone else. I will be like other Israelis, but I will also be different because I am from Ethiopia. That is a good thing."

I see that Zev is smiling. "Remember?" he says to me. "I told you that you would understand the teacher after a while." I smile back at him.

56

Soon it is time for my friends to go. They say good-bye to Papa and to Mama. Then they come to me.

"Thank you," Dani says. "It *was* special."

"You are welcome," I answer.

Zev comes to me and takes my hand in both of his, and bows to me. I think it is wonderful that he does this. Ron watches and does the same.

David leaves last. He says to me, "Your family has been so nice to us."

"Good-bye, my friends," I say, and shut the door. Mama goes into the kitchen. Papa is still at the table, thinking. I see that he looks pleased.

I go to him and he puts his arms around me. I kiss him in the Ethiopian style. And then, suddenly, all the excitement of this day makes me very tired. I say good night to my family and go to bed thinking about my new friends. Tonight I will dream about my new life in Israel.

"Rahel." I hear Papa calling to Mama. "What did I tell you? We are no longer strangers here!"

And I know that Papa is right. We are *Falasha no more*!

ABOUT THE AUTHOR

Arlene Kushner was born in Newark, N.J., 42 years ago. She has a degree in psychology from Rutgers University and has studied at the Jewish Theological Seminary.

Since 1979, one of Mrs. Kushner's prime concerns has been the plight of the Ethiopian Jews. In 1984, she spent seven months in Jerusalem, where she worked extensively with Jewish immigrants, newly arrived from Ethiopia. She is a member of the Board of Directors of the American Association for Ethiopian Jews.

Mrs. Kushner's perceptive and informative articles on Jewish subjects have appeared in such publications as *The New York Times, Outlook, The Jewish Monthly, The Baltimore Jewish Times, The Jerusalem Post* and *Reconstructionist.*

The author has written two other books for adults about the Jews of Ethiopia. *Treacherous Journey: Escape from Ethiopia* and *The Ethiopian Jews: Photographs and Letters*, they will be released in October, 1985.

Mrs. Kushner and her husband Marvin are the parents of three children. The family lives in Morris County, New Jersey, where Mrs. Kushner devotes much time to community service.